Alternative
IBS Treatments

A Research Project

Maxwell Stein

Alternative IBS Treatments
Maxwell Stein

Copyright © 2001 The Bristol Group (This Edition)
This edition published in Great Britain 2001 by
The Bristol Group Ltd,
158 Moulsham Street,
Chelmsford,
Essex CM2 0LD

ISBN 0-9537074-8-2
Typeset by SJ Design and Publishing, Bromley, Kent
Printed and bound in Great Britain by
The Guernsey Press Co. Ltd, Guernsey, C.I.

Contents

Introduction

The most common digestive problem in the Western world is a particularly uncomfortable and upsetting one. It affects some 10 per cent of people in the developed countries, usually first appearing while the sufferer is aged between 17 and 25. Two thirds of the victims who suffer from this particular syndrome are female. Also referred to as Mucous Colitis and Spastic Colon, this unpleasant disease is most often referred to as Irritable Bowel Syndrome (IBS).

IBS has a number of symptoms, not all of which are present in every case. Bowel disorders often follow family patterns, so if you suffer from an Irritable Bowel, then it is quite likely that some other members of your family also have the same problems associated with the disease. Despite this, IBS is not hereditary or catching, but given its prevalence in the Western world, it is entirely possible that if you suffer from it, then someone else in your family does, too.

The most frequent symptom of IBS is pain in the lower half of the body. This takes the form of a cramping pain that comes on in waves, and is often in the lower section of the left hand side of the abdomen, the oval area at the front of the body that reaches from the top of the pelvis (your hip-bones) to the curved line that marks the top of your ribs. The abdomen also extends some way back towards the spine. As you can appreciate, the abdomen covers a fairly wide area, and it also holds the vast majority of the digestive system. IBS can cause pain anywhere in the abdominal area, so you may feel sharp discomfort in your lower back, even. This pain may sometimes be triggered by eating, as the act of swallowing food stimulates intestinal activity.

Irritable Bowel Syndrome often produces irregularities in the process of defecation. This can manifest as either constipation or diarrhoea, although generally the two go together in cycles, with periods of constipation being followed by an uncomfortable bowel movement of hard, dry pellets of faeces, or of thin, ribbon-like stools. This movement is usually often followed by a period of diarrhoea, when all movements are thin and watery. This diarrhoea will occur more frequently in the mornings (between 5am and 10am), and, like the pains, can be triggered by eating. In either case, the faeces can contain excess amounts of an unpleasant, sticky mucus, and occasionally spots of blood. Despite the appearance given off by this, I am pleased to be able to reassure you that Irritable Bowel Syndrome absolutely does not lead to Bowel Cancer.

IBS can be a very unpleasant thing to have to suffer, but it is not life-threatening.

Another common problem that is associated with IBS is the build-up of gas in the intestines, causing pain and wind which may manifest itself as bloating, distension of the stomach and abdominal area, or as gurgling noises in the gut. The intestines are the 7 metres or so of tubing in the abdomen that mix the food you eat with acids and digestive bile, and then extract all the useful vitamins, minerals and nutrients into the body, leaving the remaining waste to be ejected as stools.

In Irritable Bowel Syndrome, the air that you normally swallow during eating and drinking can get trapped and build up inside the intestines due to their irregular movement. This leads to pain and discomfort in the stomach, feelings of bloating, and embarrassing, uncontrollable bursts of flatulence and belching. Uncontrollable wind is a very common feature of IBS, and many sufferers discover that its release actually temporarily relieves the pain that has been building up in the abdomen.

These symptoms are the ones that are classically associated with Irritable Bowel Syndrome, but to take this view overlooks many other serious problems that it can produce.

Because of the difficulties that IBS produces in actually processing food in the stomach, it can produce a variety of effects such as nausea, lack of appetite, indigestion and heartburn. The nausea can range from general feelings of queasiness to an urge to vomit, although the latter is more uncommon. Where build-up of gas occurs, many sufferers also get problems of back pains, or discover that urination is uncomfortable. Difficulty in the transfer of food along the colon can produce trouble in the absorption of sufficient nutrients for full body functioning, which can manifest itself as lack of energy, weakness and faintness; if these symptoms trouble you, try to sit or lie down and relax for a while, so as to reduce the metabolic demands of your system.

Finally, because of the inherent physical stresses of a syndrome such as IBS, you may also find that you suffer from problems more commonly associated with stress, such as heart palpitations, mental agitation, or depression. The link between stress and IBS is well identified, and I will talk more about this later, but basically these problems respond particularly well to the relaxation techniques which I will go into later, such as Pranayama Yoga, flotation and meditation, although, of course, all of the symptoms of IBS are greatly relieved by these techniques.

It is worth mentioning that many of these symptoms can also represent other stomach disorders, some of which can be quite serious. As with any self-prescribed or holistic medicinal programme, you should consult your doctor to make absolutely certain that you have made the correct diagnosis of your problem, and you should also advise him of whatever action you are taking to remedy the situation. All forms of 'alternative' medical care should be undertaken in harmony with official medical help, and never instead of – or even worse, despite – the advice of a doctor. It is a very hard thing indeed to look at yourself objectively, because you are so used to yourself that you tend to miss highly important details that an objective specialist would immediately pick up. Never make the mistake of thinking that you know your own body more accurately than a doctor would do. While this is true while you are healthy, diseases are, by definition, times when your body is acting strangely. Always see a doctor first.

Further more, it is vitally important that if your symptoms change from their normal state in any way that is not an expected result of treatment, you should contact your doctor immediately. This is particularly true for any change in the usual colour of your stools; while Irritable Bowel Syndrome is not a life-threatening disease, it shares several symptoms with illnesses that are far more dangerous. This point cannot be over-stressed. If you are in any doubt, see your doctor as soon as possible.

The level of discomfort experienced in IBS will vary from person to person, and to a lesser degree, from occasion to occasion. In its mildest forms, Irritable Bowel Syndrome can manifest as little more than frequent involuntary belching or flatulence, with the occasional spot of constipation. At its worst, IBS can be cripplingly painful, with strong and repeated stomach cramps and headaches, and the inability to eat anything without immediately having to rush to the toilet. The vast majority of cases of IBS fall between the two extremes, and it is highly unlikely that you will fall into the extremely severe category and not have already sought medical advice.

Irritable Bowel Syndrome is an extremely unpleasant disease to have to put up with. There are several things that you can do to help yourself with this problem, and I'll deal with them shortly. First, I will discuss the nature of this problem in greater depth, and explain why IBS gets as bad as it does, and how the symptoms actually arise, so as to give you a clearer picture of the enemy.

The Digestive System and IBS

In the introduction, I discussed the symptoms which can be associated with Irritable Bowel Syndrome. This, however, is no more than an explanation of what IBS can (or does) actually do to you in a day-to-day sense, and it will be useful to you to have a basic understanding of exactly what is happening to cause these unpleasant symptoms. With this in mind, I will now give you a basic introduction to the human digestive system, discussing when and how it applies to Irritable Bowel Syndrome.

You do not need to read this chapter to benefit from the advice in the rest of this book. However, I have made the discussions in here as readable as possible, and if you do choose to read it, you will gain a reasonable understanding of the way that the digestive system works, and how the procedure can be affected by Irritable Bowel Syndrome. This will give you a greater insight into the nature of IBS, and help you to understand what is happening when the syndrome takes effect.

OVER-ACTIVE INTESTINE

Nobody is completely sure about how Irritable Bowel Syndrome starts in a person. There appears to be a link between developing IBS and possessing an over-active intestine. It should be noted, however, that there is no definite causal relationship here between the two; IBS does not imply an over-active intestine, nor does an over-active intestine definitely lead to Irritable Bowel Syndrome.

STRESS

Several doctors now feel that IBS is caused by stress; this may well be an over-simplified view, but it is certain that stress plays a major part in Irritable Bowel Syndrome. Much of the treatment of IBS is centred on stress reduction and stress management. The question remains, however – what exactly is stress?

Stress is extremely difficult to define, mainly because of its wide range of both causes and effects. If pushed for a description, it could be said that stress is 'an influence, whether internal or external, that affects the day-to-day functioning of the mind and/or body'. This is obviously an extremely broad definition; it can even include things such as exercise, illnesses, and a utility bill. This may seem rather silly to you, but stop for a moment and consider it.

Unfamiliar exercise leaves you feeling tired and uncomfortable. Illness disturbs your body, and may affect your thinking and your emotions. Very few people welcome bills, and a particularly unpleasant one may well result in worry and bad temper. All of these things reduce your tolerance to other problems, and in addition to some short-term reactions, such as sweating, rapid breathing, speeding heart-beat and stiffening muscles, it can also lead to many unpleasant physical problems if the stress is long-term.

The short-term stress reactions with which most people are familiar – think of how you feel when angry or scared – are the direct result of the adrenal gland, located at the top of the kidney, releasing hormones designed to allow the body to function at maximum physical efficiency in case of danger. These hormones are adrenalin and noradrenalin. These are only triggered by severe, immediate stress.

In the case of long-term stress, such as is caused by hating the work that you do, so that you dread getting up in the mornings, cortisol is released into the body by the adrenal gland, which increases the availability of blood sugar in your system, providing more available energy. This is achieved by breaking down amino acids in the blood. In addition, aldosterone, also released by the adrenal gland, maintains a blood pressure that is higher than normal, allowing the body's chemical system to react more efficiently to the demands of the blood circulation systems.

Unsurprisingly, long periods of high blood pressure and decreased quantities of amino acids – the body's building-blocks – do not contribute to general good health, and physical deficiencies will start to crop up.

Stress, whether short-term or long-term, will make it harder for your body to deal with any medical problem, aggravating the disorder, and also increasing the level of stress you are under. With Irritable Bowel Syndrome, because the digestive system is very reactive to external conditions, stress nearly always plays a major role in the aggravation of IBS symptoms, worsening the disorder.

Whether stress is actually the cause of IBS or merely a contributing factor is still uncertain, but doctors have been unable to locate any definite reason why Irritable Bowel Syndrome should develop in a specific person. IBS responds very positively to stress management techniques, as well as to other forms of treatment, and I will give you some tried and tested methods for reducing the stress in your life. Before that, however, let's have a look at the digestive system.

HOW THE DIGESTIVE SYSTEM WORKS

Although it might seem an obvious point, the human digestive system serves the purpose of breaking down the food that is consumed in the body into its constituent nutrients by mixing it with strong digestive acids in the stomach. The resulting mix is then passed into the minor and major intestines, and once processed, is deposited in the bowels for excretion. This process takes both chemical and physical action on the part of the body; chemical to extract the nutrients out of the food as soluble products, and physical to move the food through the body as it is processed.

From mouth to anus, the tube that the food travels through is known as the alimentary canal. This is obviously divided into many separate sections, such as the mouth and oesophagus, the stomach, the intestines and the bowels. Digestion starts when food is chewed in the mouth, grinding it into small pieces, and mixing it with saliva, which moistens it and begins breaking down some of the food.

The food then travels down the oesophagus, and is carried down to the stomach by the wavelike motions of the alimentary canal, a process known as peristalsis. This movement carries the food along for the entire time that it is in the digestive system, and Irritable Bowel Syndrome is caused by the failure of the intestines to co-ordinate the peristalsis properly, causing the constipation/diarrhoea, and the build-up of gas. Peristalsis is a completely involuntary process, beyond conscious control.

The oesophagus meets the stomach at a sphincter

valve, a muscle that lets the food in when appropriate, and stops any from re-entering the oesophagus; when this fails to co-ordinate properly, you can get severe heartburn, as the oesophagus is not as well able to cope with the stomach acids as the stomach lining is.

The food in the stomach is churned in with enzymes, acid and mucus, generated by millions of small glands in the stomach lining. Up to 3 litres of gastric juices (the general name for the digestive fluids in the stomach) are produced every day.

The combination of food, enzymes and acids reduces the food to a thick liquid known as chyme, which is then passed through another sphincter muscle into the small intestine. This muscle also further crushes the chyme, and when working properly, controls the rate at which the chyme is passed into the intestine. This too can malfunction in IBS, causing a variety of symptoms such as indigestion, heartburn and lack of appetite.

In general, it takes food between 30 and 40 hours to travel from mouth to anus, along the length of the alimentary canal. Different foods get processed at different rates; sugars and starches are processed far more rapidly than proteins, and fat stays around for longer still.

This is the reason why heavy, fatty meals are more satisfying to consume than vegetables, fruit or sweets, and also why certain dietary constraints can help reduce the effect of Irritable Bowel Syndrome. The stomach is not actually vital to life; in extreme circumstances, the small intestine can do all the work that the stomach normally would.

THE SMALL INTESTINE

The small intestine is the longest single part of the alimentary canal, stretching to between 6.5 and 7.5 metres in length. In normal digestion, food is held in this area for several hours. The liver and the pancreas connect to the intestine by small tubes – ducts – through which they secrete further digestive fluids into the small intestine.

The fluids which come from the pancreas, which is one of the most important glands in the body, specifically break down proteins, carbohydrates and fats. This digestive fluid contains enzymes which help digest carbohydrates, proteins and fats into sugars, amino acids and fatty acids respectively. The liver contributes bile to the chyme, which has no specific digestive purpose, but generally aids the process.

By the time that the chyme has passed through the small intestine, most of the nutrients in it have been absorbed into the walls of the small intestine. In the case of Irritable Bowel Syndrome, the chyme is not passed through the body at an even rate. This moderately affects the nutritional absorption, but because the food passes relatively rapidly through the small intestine, the effects of IBS in the small intestine are much less than the effects in the large intestine. It should be noted that the small intestine is considerably longer than the large intestine – over 6 metres, in fact, it makes up the huge majority of the alimentary canal.

THE LARGE INTESTINE

Once the chyme has entered the large intestine, which is approximately 2.5 metres long, it takes between 10 and 20 hours to be processed in a fully healthy intestine, and in cases of Irritable Bowel Syndrome, the time taken can vary wildly from very short – producing diarrhoea – through to very long, leading to constipation.

The large intestine serves to remove the majority of the water from the processed chyme, so that it becomes the solids that we recognise as faeces. Once mainly solidified, the waste is deposited into the descending colon, the final section of the large intestine, to await excretion via the semi-voluntary anal sphincter muscle.

The majority of the common symptoms of IBS arise at this stage, where the system of peristalsis, already very slow in the large intestine, becomes erratic. If the process is too fast, diarrhoea is excreted due to excess water in the stools; if the process is too slow, too much water is removed, and the constipation produced by the delay in excretion, when finally relieved, produces dry, hard pellets that are generally painful to pass. As mucus is produced all along the alimentary canal, it can build up in areas of unusually slow movement during IBS, leading to excess deposits of mucus on the faeces, which can occur during both the diarrhoea and constipation forms of IBS.

SECTION 2

The Diet and IBS

If you read the previous chapter, you will have some understanding of the way the body processes different types of food. To recap, the stomach disposes of some foods more rapidly that it does others. Specifically, sugars and starches are rapidly taken into the body, so foods rich in these tend to get digested rapidly.

Foods with high fibre and roughage contents tend to get moved swiftly through the digestive tracts because they are bulky, and so give the muscular contractions in the digestive system something to grip securely, and thus get processed rapidly.

Protein, which needs to be broken down into amino acids, takes a fair amount longer to exit the stomach, and longer again to move through the intestines. The food type that remains longest in the system is fat, because it is in a form that the body uses specifically to store energy in against long-term needs, and so needs more time to be broken down.

In many cases, consuming foods that are processed more rapidly will help with the regularity of the digestive system, but as there are plenty of exceptions, I will go into this in greater detail.

MORE FIBRE

In general, the dietary changes that will help relieve Irritable Bowel Syndrome are ones that would normally be associated with moving from a normal, Western daily diet to a healthy, wholefood diet. Fibre and roughage are very important to the regular functioning of the digestive system, because they swell up in the intestines as they absorb water, and aid the process of peristalsis, the movement of food through the digestive system. Eating plenty of fibre will mean that, even with your intestines pushing the food along erratically or weakly, it stays more evenly spaced and moves at a more normal pace, helping to avoid constipation and diarrhoea, and the pains that they bring with them.

Increasing the amount of fibre in your diet is both simple and tasty. Try to avoid pre-packed and processed foods, and purchase their natural equivalents. Instead of buying white bread or rice, obtain wholewheat bread and whole brown rice; because of the extra parts that these foods contain, that are removed during the bleaching process, the level of fibre is significantly higher. In addition to this, white bread and rice often contain many chemicals, flavourings and preservatives that are not present in wholefood varieties.

At breakfast time, eat a fibre-rich natural breakfast, such as muesli or porridge, rather than buttered toast or an additive-rich breakfast cereal. Muesli is particularly good as it tends to include a variety of fibre and roughage from several different sources. You can also increase your fibre intake by eating fresh fruit, particularly apricots and figs, and other vegetable foods such as nuts, seeds, peas, sweetcorn and beans. All of these are high in fibre, and will help reduce the effects of an irritable bowel.

PLEASE NOTE

In approximately one quarter of IBS sufferers, increasing the bran/fibre intake will actually increase the levels of discomfort felt. This increase will last for no more than two weeks, after which the benefits of the new diet will start to become apparent as pain and bloating fade to far lower than they were before the new eating patterns were started. Basically, the message here is persevere; if a higher fibre intake starts to make you feel worse, do not give it up, and within 14 days you will be delighted that you stuck with it.

REDUCE SATURATED FATS

Another dietary change that you can make is to reduce the amount of heavy, saturated fat that you consume. Fat takes much longer to process in the stomach than starches and sugars, longer, in fact, than any other food group.

Fat also takes a lot of processing in the intestines, and because it dissolves into the gastric fluids, it provides nothing whatsoever for the intestine walls to grip during peristalsis, increasing the load on intestines, and also making you more susceptible to the symptoms of Irritable Bowel Syndrome. Some vegetable oils are much lighter than most fats, however, so there is no need to give up fats altogether.

Dairy products are often very high in saturated fats; the worst are butter, cream, cheese and whole (or worse, cream-enriched) milk. There are plenty of excellent substitutes for these substances, however. Instead of fatty butter, there are many polyunsaturated margarines available on the market. If you can find one made with olive oil, so much the better. Olive oil is not only a light, quickly processed fat, but it has actually been shown to help in the reduction of cholesterol in the bloodstream, reducing the load on your heart.

The switch to cooking with olive oil rather than other forms of oil cannot be recommended enough. It may cost slightly more, but it is far better for you than most other oils and, in addition, it has a wonderful flavour that complements most fried foods. Many countries consider bread dipped in olive oil to be a delicious snack; can you imagine the same being true of a tasteless corn oil? To help cut the price down, I can reassure you that there is no need to purchase extra virgin olive oil. All this means is that the oil was produced from the first pressing of the olives, rather than any subsidiary pressings. The flavour is slightly stronger, and the aroma is more pungent.

You can also use substitutes for other dairy products. Fromage frais can be used as a very pleasant and healthy substitute for cream, and will cope happily with most situations that you would use cream for. Fromage frais is light and tasty, and will give your intestines far less trouble than thick cream. If you are going to use it in a sweet dish, or eat it on its own, it is often worth getting a small amount of a soft fruit, such as peaches, strawberries or kiwi fruit, and chopping into the fromage frais, adding a delicious texture and flavour.

Many sufferers of Irritable Bowel Syndrome find that live yoghurt is a very helpful dairy food to eat. Unlike the pre-packed, chemical-filled commercial yoghurts, where all the bacteria have been killed, so that you are basically consuming a thick, flavoured liquid; in live yoghurt the bacteria are still very much active. These bacteria are fully compatible with the ones in the human digestive system, and so when you eat live yoghurt, the bacteria that it contains will line the alimentary canal – the channel that food passes through between mouth and anus – and aid in both the effective digestion of food and the regularity of its processing. Merely consuming live yoghurt can help to relieve the problems associated with Irritable Bowel Syndrome, although I am not suggesting that *just eating live yoghurt* is a sensible way to go about treating the problem.

AVOID RED MEAT

You should also try to avoid red meat. The red meats all have a high level of unsaturated fat in them, and are heavy on the stomach, taking a fair amount of time to process. By putting strain on the intestines, they can worsen the problems of IBS. Note that pork and veal, although they cook to white, are also red meats, and ought to be cut down on.

A sensible alternative is to eat more fish and poultry, where this is possible; these foods are lighter than red meats, and in general contain less fat. Particularly fatty fish and fowl, such as mackerel, shark and duck, ought to be viewed with a certain degree of caution.

Just as important is how the meat is actually cooked. Roasting and frying allow the meat to not only retain its natural fats, but also to absorb more from the oil during cooking. Where possible, grill instead of fry, and bake instead of roast. This allows the fat inside the meat to drain off during cooking, making it far less of a strain for your digestive system. This is particularly true for grilling, and if you absolutely have to eat very high-fat meats such as bacon and sausage, try to ensure that they have been grilled. The difference in terms of fat content between a fried sausage and a well-grilled sausage is staggering.

HERBS AND SPICES

There are several herbs and spices which have a calming effect on the stomach and digestive process. It is well worth working these into your daily diet as food additives, garnishes or herbal teas.

Marjoram, dill, rosemary and clove all add an interesting flavour when worked into cookery, particularly rosemary with meats, dill with fish and clove in hot sweets. Black pepper and parsley can be very successfully added to the majority of meals as a garnish or during cooking.

Aniseed, peppermint and spearmint go very well with several sweet dishes, and along with camomile, fennel and lemon balm can often be found as herbal teas. Particularly useful are combination teas, such as camomile and peppermint, or lemon balm and fennel. All of these teas are very soothing, and make a delicious mid-morning drink.

These herbs and spices will all help your digestive system to relax and function more naturally, and camomile has been a well-known herbal remedy to several complaints for hundreds of years. Working these herbs and spices into your everyday diet will have greatly helpful effects in relieving the symptoms of Irritable Bowel Syndrome, and further more, the effects they have will be completely natural and work without subjecting your body to stress.

VITAMINS AND MINERALS

There are also several vitamins and minerals that you can add to your diet in order to help reduce the effects of stress on your body, and so alleviate IBS. Every vitamin has a different specific effect on the body, and it is frankly unrealistic in the modern world to hope that a daily diet will be able to provide the necessary levels of vitamins and minerals for a person to function properly, given the stresses of the way of life that we lead.

Vitamin B-complex

Vitamin B, one of the more important anti-stress vitamins, is in fact a group of vitamins, known collectively as the vitamin B-complex. Many of the B-complex vitamins directly affect the functioning of the adrenal glands and the central nervous system, often protecting against damage to the nerves or producing a relaxant effect. Adequate dosage of these vitamins can help reduce stress and nervous exhaustion, and so alleviate the symptoms of Irritable Bowel Syndrome.

The Vitamin B-complex is made up of the following vitamins:

- B_1 (thiamine) – needed for the nerves to work properly
- B_2 (riboflavin) – aids the function of the nervous system
- B_3 (niacin/niacinamide) – produces calmness
- B_5 (pantothenic acid) – vital to adrenal glands

- B_6 (pyridoxine) – needed by adrenal glands and nerves
- B_{12} (cyanocobalamin) – protects nerve endings

In addition, the following B-complex vitamins are also needed in order to avoid depression, irritability, listlessness and insomnia:
- PABA (parabenzoic acid)
- folic acid
- biotin
- inositol
- choline

A good vitamin B-complex supplement will contain between 50 and 100mg of most of the B vitamins, along with considerably smaller doses of B_{12}, biotin and folic acid. It may be necessary to obtain extra B_5 (pantothenic acid), as somewhere around 200mg per day might be needed when the body is stressed. B_5 is not only an essential vitamin (necessary to ensure survival), but it is also practically non-toxic at very high dosage, so do not be too concerned about taking higher doses of it.

Vitamin C

Vitamin C is also absolutely vital to the body, both under stress and in normal living conditions. It has a huge range of functions, strengthening artery walls, reducing cholesterol and fat in the bloodstream, stimulating the immune system, allowing collagen production (collagen, a connective tissue, is the body's most common protein) and most significantly of all, perhaps, allowing the adrenal glands to function correctly.

As vitamin C (ascorbic acid) is not really stored in the body, but processed quickly and the excess ejected, a reasonable daily intake would be 1000 to 1500mg, spread over the day. It is commonly purchased in pleasantly-flavoured chewing tablets of 500mg, and one of these with each meal will greatly enhance the ability of the body to cope with stress, as well as increasing the overall level of health. In terms of Irritable Bowel Syndrome, a good intake of vitamin C can go a long way to holding off the disorder, both by reducing stress and by helping in the body's self-healing processes.

Zinc, Magnesium, Calcium and Potassium

In addition to these two major vitamins, zinc, magnesium, calcium and potassium are all very important in the handling of stress. Zinc and magnesium are both very important to the adrenal glands in the production of the various adrenal secretions. Along with calcium, they also have several very important roles to play in the correct functioning of the nervous system. Potassium is needed throughout the entire body to ensure correct balances of all the bodily cells.

All four of these minerals are depleted rapidly under stress, and so supplements of them can greatly help the body to cope with stress, and in doing so reduce the effects of Irritable Bowel Syndrome. Remember, it is always advisable to consult your doctor, but in general, for a highly-stressed adult, up to a maximum of 30mg of zinc, 500mg of magnesium, 2000mg of potassium and 1000mg of calcium might be necessary. At least half of this dosage is recommended for mild stress. These doses are likely to be unavailable in a multimineral/multivitamin supplement, so you may consider obtaining them separately.

A daily dietary supplement of vitamin B-complex, vitamin C, zinc, magnesium, calcium and potassium, each obtained separately to the suggested dosage, will have a greatly beneficial effect on the levels of stress that you suffer. In doing so it will greatly ease Irritable Bowel Syndrome, particularly if used in conjunction with the other dietary recommendations suggested in this chapter. For many people, following the suggestions in this chapter will eliminate IBS completely, without recourse to other forms of treatment.

AVOID GASSY FOODS AND DRINKS

As many of the problems associated with Irritable Bowel Syndrome are aggravated by internal build-up of gas, particularly the bloating, flatulence and belching, it is well worth trying to avoid gassy foods and drinks. In particular, chewing-gum and bubble-gum should not be used, and if possible you should try to avoid fizzy drinks. Gas-producing vegetables, such as cabbage and artichokes, might also be worth cutting out of your diet. If you are particularly prone to wind problems, you ought to also consider avoiding beans and legumes.

Many types of alcoholic drink contain large amounts of carbon dioxide, which will only make your problems worse. Beers, ciders and sparkling wines are particularly bad for gas content. If you are going to consume alcohol, the best form that you can take it in is red wine. As well as being free from extra gas, there is some evidence that in moderation it can actually help your long-term health. A good red wine will not be overloaded with unpleasant chemicals, unlike the vast majority of beers and ciders, and will not only help your liver to purge itself of undesirable built-up secretions, but also may help to reduce blood cholesterol in much the same way that olive oil does.

You ought to know that alcohol in general stimulates the production of adrenalin in the body, however, in much the same way as stress does, so the less alcohol that you consume, the less aggravated Irritable Bowel Syndrome will become.

CAFFEINE

Alcohol is not the only drug that makes IBS worse. Caffeine has a very similar effect to alcohol, speeding up your metabolism, stimulating adrenalin production, and in general increasing the levels of internal stress on your body. I discussed earlier the ways in which stress adversely affects Irritable Bowel Syndrome; not only does it make the problem many times worse than it might otherwise be, some doctors even think that it causes the syndrome in the first place.

Several of the healing methods that I will detail later are designed primarily to reduce your personal stress levels, and this form of treatment has proven remarkably successful in alleviating the symptoms of Irritable Bowel Syndrome, and even removing them completely.

NICOTINE

Nicotine is another substance that has a very poor effect on Irritable Bowel Syndrome. Highly addictive, amongst other dreadful effects it has on your body, nicotine also increases the levels of adrenalin in the body. In non-smokers, a cigarette will produce a 'rush'; this feeling is caused directly by the triggering of a large adrenalin secretion from the adrenal glands. In long-term smokers, the effect is a relaxant. This is because the adrenal glands have been so badly damaged that they can no longer release useful levels of adrenalin without the help of nicotine, and so the body becomes unable to deal with any stressors without external nicotine, leaving the smoker greatly discomforted until a cigarette can be smoked. In both cases, the effect is to greatly enhance the damaging effects of stress on the body, and to thus worsen IBS.

As if this wasn't enough, the nicotine also directly affects the digestive system by interfering with peristalsis, causing the intestines to spasmodically constrict. It should be obvious that anything which further upsets the natural operation of the intestines can only further aggravate Irritable Bowel Syndrome. Whilst smoking is very hard to give up, any smoker who is serious about beating IBS should attempt to stop, or at the very least, cut down greatly on their daily intake of nicotine.

Following these dietary recommendations will, in many cases, completely remove all traces of Irritable Bowel Syndrome, as well as greatly increasing your overall health, and leading to a state of general well-being. At the very least, it will greatly reduce the problems that IBS causes.

SECTION 3

Relaxation Techniques and IBS

There are many relaxation techniques that are available to people quickly and easily. They all work in much the same way; by allowing the mind and body to relax, the person becomes physically and mentally refreshed, and more importantly, the level of internal stress is greatly reduced, allowing clearer thinking about stressful situations, a greater facility to cope with problems, and removing the harmful pressures on the body which cause so much damage. As so many cases of IBS seem to be stress-related, relaxational techniques can form a very important cure for the syndrome, and will certainly reduce the discomfort associated with the problem.

In this chapter, I am going to detail three different relaxation techniques. Although there are many others, these three cover most of the spectrum of possible methods, and at least one of them should appeal to the majority of people. In addition, it is my personal opinion that these three methods are the best forms of relaxation.

1. MEDITATION

The first of these, perhaps the simplest of all relaxation techniques, and definitely one of the most effective, is meditation. Once you strip the mystical material out of meditation, you are left with what can be described as 'letting your mind wander without thought'. People often have many misconceptions about meditation – that it is dangerous, or difficult, or about self-improvement, or journeying to perfection. It can be all these things, if you use it in specific ways, but basically meditation is just a way of letting your mind relax. Meditation is as simple and easy as it is helpful.

To actually perform a meditation, the only thing that you really need is some time to yourself. Although you can even meditate successfully while standing in a noisy, crowded commuter train on your way to work if you have had some practice, the best conditions for meditation are somewhere quiet and pleasant, where you are not going to be disturbed. If background noise intrudes on you, try putting on some relaxing music to help block it out. Your clothes should be ones that you are comfortable in, and do not distract you.

If you are feeling tired, you should sit in a comfortable chair, but if you are not weary, it is better to lie down, either on a bed or on a mat on the floor. Whichever way you choose, your body should be in a basically open posture, with all your limbs away from each other. If you are lying down, lie flat on your back with your legs out and your arms fairly straight, slightly away from your sides. Your hands should be slightly cupped. If you are sitting, rest your head comfortably and try to sit basically upright with your legs uncrossed and your hands resting on your thighs.

Overall, the important thing is that you should feel comfortable, and able to stay in the position for up to 30 minutes, depending on how much free time you have. Of course, if you wish to meditate for longer than this, that's fine. Meditation is as inherently dangerous as dozing or watching television, and is only a sensible and healthy alternative to both.

To begin a meditation, close your eyes, and feel your whole body relax. The best way to do this is to imagine your body filled up with water to bursting point, pressing against your skin, making you tense and taut all over. The feeling should be slightly uncomfortable, and make you want to tense your muscles, but it should not be worrying. If you start getting nervous that you might burst, you are (a) naturally very good at meditation and (b) taking it too far!

Once you can feel this tension throughout your body, imagine the water slowly draining away, either through your feet if you are sitting down, or through your back if you are lying down. As it drains away, your whole body relaxes, sagging back into a comfortable, peaceful state. Once all that water has drained away, you will be left feeling physically relaxed and comfortable.

Keep your eyes closed; in fact, they should stay closed during the entire meditative session. If you need to blink or twitch, do so. There is no need to get concerned about staying absolutely still.

When the water has drained, you are ready to start actually meditating. Think of a place or time in your life when you have been happy and without worries. This may be back in your childhood bedroom, or it may be a favourite lake, or anything. As long as you felt peaceful and happy at that place and time, then that is all that is required. Start imagining the place as it was, and its surroundings. Everything is peaceful and calm, and there is nothing there that bothers you. Take your time, and just wander around the place that you have re-created, looking at things, and just feeling the warmth, love and peace of the place.

If any thoughts rise up into your mind, thoughts from your everyday life, just note to yourself that they have arisen, then let them fall back down out of your special place. You can think about them later, when it is the right time. If you find that your mind has been wandering, and you suddenly notice it, don't worry about it, just patiently rebuild the scene you were visiting, over and over if needs be.

As time goes on, you will find fewer and fewer distractions and wanderings intrude into your meditation. Stay here, looking around and enjoying the feelings, for as long as you want. You may occasionally find things or people that you do not remember, or did not intend to be there. It doesn't matter in the slightest. Look at them, talk to them if you want, and if you are even slightly bothered by them, just note that they appeared, turn your back on them and go a different way. These stray images are produced by the unconscious mind, and may often have a helpful meaning to you, but don't worry about it during the meditation, think back on it afterwards.

When you have spent enough time in your place, think about your body, and yourself in it. Pay full attention to your surroundings again, wriggle your fingers and toes slightly so as to bring your mind back to your body, and then open your eyes and get up. If the images were very faintly remembered, or you kept getting disturbed by the world around you, don't worry about it. The meditation will still have had a good effect on you, and the clarity of the imagination will get stronger as you continue doing it.

You don't have to stay in one place, either. If you get bored with one imagined place, simply wipe that location away from your mind, and start with another one. It is usually best to start with a specific object or scene that you can picture clearly, and then increasing your viewpoint from there.

And that is all there is to performing a pleasant, relaxing, stress-relieving meditation. It's a lovely, therapeutic way of spending half an hour or so.

2. PRANIC BREATHING

The next method of relaxation that I want to tell you about is derived from Pranayama Yoga, or Pranic Breathing. Basically, this involves sitting down and breathing deeply for a period of time; not a particularly arduous task. Despite its simplicity, Pranic Breathing will not only relax you completely, it will also tone the nervous system, aid the digestive process in its entirety, massage the intestinal area, increase clarity of thought, and can relieve depressive, worried or melancholy moods. Part of this can be attributed to the increased flow of oxygen into the bloodstream, particularly the mental and nervous effects, but because of the way it rhythmically moves the abdomen, it also has strongly positive effects on the digestive system and the intestines. This is an extra benefit to Irritable Bowel Syndrome sufferers from what is basically a relaxational technique.

Unlike the meditation, there are some guidelines to follow in preparing yourself for a session of Pranayama Yoga that will allow greater efficiency in breathing deeply and smoothly. To begin with, you should not have performed any vigorous exercise for at least an hour before the yoga. To have the body either tired or already oxygenated is not desirable for this form of relaxation. Further more, your stomach should be relatively empty; allow an hour after a snack, and two hours after a meal. If the stomach is full, it will hamper the expansion of the lungs, making deep breathing difficult.

You should sit in a clean, pleasant, well-ventilated room with no unpleasant odours, wearing as little slack-fitting clothing as you need to feel comfortable or avoid causing offence. If circumstances permit, nudity is best, because this allows your skin full access to the outside air, so that the pores can also breathe. When all is said and done, however, it is better to be comfortable and clothed than uncomfortable and unclothed. Empty your bladder before beginning the breathing, wash your hands and face, and also blow several times down each nostril to ensure that they are clear. If you are unable to breathe through your nostrils, then you may breathe through your mouth, but you will get a far more even and steady airflow through your nose.

In all Pranayama work, the posture that you take should be an immobile seated position. You should sit on the floor with your legs crossed, back straight, head held level, and the back, neck and head in a vertical line. The backs of your hands should rest on your knees, with your palm slightly curled inwards. For the sake of comfort, I recommend sitting on a cushion or a mat. If you find yourself unable to keep this pose for 10 minutes, then sit tight up against a wall. In this posture, none of your internal organs are cramped up against each other, with your lungs, ribs, thoracic cage and abdomen all free of pressures, and able to move as necessary. This allows for natural, free movement of the body during both inhalation and exhalation.

Actual practice of the breathing is simple. Close your eyes, and breathe smoothly and steadily through your nostrils until your lungs are full. Do not hurry this, as smooth regularity is more important than speed. To maximise this, you should picture your lungs as having three sections – which, of course, they do not – dividing up into bottom, middle and top. As you breathe in, picture the bottom section filling up with air first, then the middle section, and finally the top. You should not breathe in so much air that it becomes uncomfortable, only breathe in until you feel that your lungs are comfortably full. As you do so, really focus your attention on the act of inhaling, on how your nostrils, throat and lungs feel. It is a good idea to count how long it takes you to fill your lungs, and then make sure that this is the length of time for which you breathe in (and out) each time you take a breath.

Once your lungs are full, you then hold your breath in the lungs for a fairly short amount of time. Four seconds is a reasonable level to begin with. If this makes you feel uncomfortable, then do not hold your breath for so long. Do make sure that you hold your breath for the same amount of time each time. During this period, be very aware of the feelings inside your lungs and throughout your body as you count off the time for the hold. If you have over-filled your lungs, you will notice it at this stage as discomfort.

After you have held your lungs full, release the air back through your nostrils at the same rate that you inhaled it, steadily and smoothly again, trying to take the same amount of time to exhale as you did to inhale. Start from the imaginary lower section of the lungs again, and see the breath moving upwards, and streaming steadily out of the nostrils. Again, you should not try to empty your lungs so strongly that you experience any discomfort, merely until you have performed a comfortable complete exhalation. As it is not physically possible to actually totally fill or totally empty the lungs voluntarily, you should not try to achieve this.

As I mentioned earlier, you should attempt to synchronise the length of time that it takes to breathe out with the length of time that it took to breathe in. This will get much more accurate as you continue practising. You should be very aware of the feelings of your lungs emptying and shrinking, and the feeling of the breath leaving your body. Some practitioners also recommend imagining the breath leaving your body as being darkened and cloudy with impurities and imperfections that you are ejecting, and the air that you are inhaling as clear and sparkling, and glowing with a warm white energy. In practice, this little mental trick can leave you feeling more invigorated and healthy at the end of the session, so you may consider it worth doing if you find visualisation of this sort relatively easy to cope with.

The final part of the exercise is to hold your lungs empty for as long as you held them full. Once again, this should not be done to a stage that produces actual discomfort, so if you find that you cannot hold empty lungs as long as you can hold full ones, then cut back on both times until both holds are comfortable. It is important for the sake of balance that both time periods are the same; this allows the body to continue the breathing exercise for longer periods of time without you starting to get dizzy. If you do feel yourself beginning to get dizzy, just stop the breathing exercise for a minute or so, until the spell passes. Once again, make sure to pay very close attention to the sensations involved in holding your breath.

Once you have finished the empty holding stage, start breathing in again. You should be aiming to achieve 4 or 5 breaths a minute in this fashion, and every minute or so you should breathe normally for 15 to 20 seconds. This Pranic Breathing should be continued for 10 minutes, once a day. After a couple of weeks, you may try to extend the periods of holding your breath (both in and out concurrently) if you feel like it; the goal to aim for in this instance is for you to breathe in, hold, breathe out and hold for the same amount of time, but this will take two or three months to achieve. Remember that under no circumstances should you push yourself to the point of feeling uncomfortable.

After a session of Pranic Breathing, you will feel refreshed, invigorated and cheerful. It will also have greatly reduced the levels of short-term stress that you are experiencing, and also have gently stimulated your digestive system to more normal operation, calming and relaxing it.

3. FLOTATION THERAPY

The final form of relaxation that I am going to discuss is slightly different from the others in that you cannot practically perform it on your own, and this is Flotation Therapy.

Flotation involves being completely isolated from the world, so that no external sensory input can get to you. The way that this is achieved is quite clever. Wearing a bathing costume, you are put into a large tank of water that contains enough minerals to keep you floating on the top. Both the water and the air above it are at body temperature. In some centres, you are given breathing equipment for times when you might want to turn face-down. Regardless of this, your eyes are blocked, sometimes to dark, and sometimes to a soft, retinal red with the aid of small light diffusers.

In addition, your ears are blocked, usually by playing soft white noise into them. White noise consists of random-length bursts of sounds chosen again at random from across the entire audible spectrum, many at a time. The result is a bland hiss which very rapidly becomes completely ignored by the brain, and also blocks out all other sound, which just drops into the random mélange and vanishes. This also has the advantage of quieting all the little internal noises, such as breathing or moving your joints. This combination of eyes blocked by red light, and ears by white noise, is known in some scientific circles as the Ganzfeld state, after a researcher who first used it to isolate patients from all external influence.

Once in the tank, the water cushions you from feelings of weight, effectively blocking out gravity. You can hear nothing, see nothing, and if you lie still with your arms and legs out (as usually advised), you will rapidly not feel anything, either.

This isolation may not sound particularly pleasant to you, but in fact it is one of the most relaxing sensations that can be found, as your brain makes use of the time to completely unwind. I am not exaggerating in the slightest when I say that if done regularly, Flotation Therapy can completely revolutionise your life. It is generally impractical to consider more than one 30-minute session of Flotation a week, and much less than this will reduce the benefits of the therapy. If you look at the alternative health adverts for your area, you will find that most major towns have a Flotation centre.

RELAXATION SUMMARY

All of the techniques in this chapter approach the problem of Irritable Bowel System obliquely, by reducing stress, and giving your body some space to work on itself. You may feel that a more direct attack would be more effective than this, but don't be fooled. Most people will find that any one of these techniques will go a very long way towards eradicating IBS from their life. The same holds true for more active forms of therapy that follow this chapter; they are all extremely effective. Really, it is a matter of personal preference as to which methods you choose to relieve the symptoms, although I do advise adopting the dietary changes recommended in the previous chapter as well as one of the other therapy techniques.

Self-Hypnosis and IBS

The word 'Hypnosis' frightens a good many people without any real reason. Derived from the Greek words 'Hypnos' (Sleep) and 'Gnosis' (Knowledge), it literally means 'The Knowing Sleep'. Popular media has spent a lot of time in the last 20 years terrifying the public with a range of tales of hypnosis, from stories of psychologists doing horrible and unspeakable things to people while they are in a trance, to bad B-movies of killer hypnotists, to rumour and urban folklore of the 'A cousin of my friend got hypnotised and NEVER WOKE UP!' variety.

These stories are, of course, ridiculous. While it is true that there are a very few evil-minded psychologists who have raped hypnotised patients, or implanted false memories, hypnosis itself is as dangerous as sleeping. When you are hypnotised, you are prone to believe what you are told. This belief does not take effect in the conscious mind, but in the subconscious mind, where you hold memories, and where all the 'automatic' functions of your body are controlled. It is only during hypnosis that the subconscious mind can be consciously accessed. When this part of your mind believes something, it will ensure that reality conforms to what it believes rather than change the belief.

Think about that last sentence. The part of your mind which controls all your automatic functions will change your body to fit what it believes to be true. The applications of hypnosis in healing are therefore immense. There are some safety checks built in. If a hypnotic suggestion goes against the interests, beliefs or morals of the subject, then not only will it be ignored, but the subject will either wake up, or go truly to sleep, as mental conflict will break the trance. Contrary to popular belief, it is not possible to make someone do something that they would not do under normal circumstances.

In self-hypnosis, things are made even safer, partly because the level of trance is much lighter, and partly because you are the one who is giving you the commands. Only a psychotic would hypnotise themselves into doing something that they really had no desire to do!

If you do not tell yourself to wake up, then after a fairly short period of time, you will either wake up naturally, or go to sleep and then wake up naturally. There is no way whatsoever that you can get stuck in a trance for much more than 30 minutes.

WARNING: *There is one note of caution that I ought to sound. You will quickly understand exactly how self-hypnosis works when you have finished reading this chapter, and you may well feel like using it for other purposes as well as helping you with your IBS. This is fine; I encourage you to do so. Self-hypnosis can quickly and easily stop long-term pain, and when you become proficient, it will stop immediate pain, too. However, there is one thing to bear in mind. Pain is a warning to you from your body that something is damaged and needs attention. This means that if you start feeling a pain or ache somewhere, and you are not completely certain what is causing the pain, you should go and see a doctor, not blot the pain out. It is perfectly possible to wake up with a sore throat, hypnotise the pain away, and then feel nothing until your tonsils burst and you are rushed to the emergency ward.*

If you know why the pain is there – IBS, for example, or the bit of glass sticking into your thumb, or whatever, then the use of self-hypnosis is extremely sensible. Mysterious, unfamiliar or new pains ought to be left alone. Take some painkillers, and if the pain does not go away, seek medical advice. Once the source of the pain is known, then use self-hypnosis all you like. Many pregnant women have used self-hypnosis to give themselves a comfortable, painless childbirth.

Self-hypnosis consists of putting yourself into a light trance, repeating some commands to yourself, and then coming back out of the trance. Perfectly simple, really. As a beginner, you will not feel much difference while you are in the trance, if any at all. Each time you perform a self-hypnotism, the trance gets more effective and deeper, and comes on more rapidly.

Nowadays, I am able to put myself into a light trance by taking and then exhaling a single breath, and a deep trance takes about 30 seconds. It is all a matter of practice.

Before you begin a session of self-hypnosis, it is better for your body to be in a state that will not disturb you. These strictures are similar to the ones for getting prepared for Pranic Breathing, as explained in the last chapter. Put simply and briefly, you should wear light, comfortable clothing that will not bother you in any way. The room should be light, airy and clean, with no unpleasant odours. Background noise should be as little as possible, and you should try to guarantee that you will not be interrupted by anyone. If you are interrupted, you will merely wake up, but you will then have to start the self-hypnosis from the beginning. Empty your bladder before you start, and if you feel it will help, put on some quiet, relaxing music and/or light a stick of incense.

You may either be seated or lying down for self-hypnosis. You should be comfortable enough to remain still for 30 minutes or so, but you should not be so comfortable that you go to sleep. If sitting, you should sit upright, with no parts of your body folded or crossed, and your back straight. Your hands should be resting palms down on your knees. If you are lying down, then lie out straight, with your legs together and your arms in by your sides, your hands palms downwards, and slightly cupped.

Once you are comfortable, close your eyes. Bring an image of yourself in your mind, and then say:

"My Left Foot is completely relaxed."

As you do so, imagine the foot glowing with a soft, warming white light. Actually feel your foot being warm, tingly and relaxed. Hold this for a second, and then proceed left to right, up your body as follows:

"My Right Foot is completely relaxed."

See it glowing with the warming white light, feel it warmed and relaxed, and pause.

"My Left Ankle is completely relaxed."

See the glow. Feel the warm relaxation.

"My Right Ankle is completely relaxed."

See the glow. Feel the warm relaxation.

"My Lower Left Leg is completely relaxed."

See the glow. Feel the warm relaxation.

"My Lower Right Leg is completely relaxed."

See the glow. Feel the warm relaxation.

"My Left Knee is completely relaxed."

See the glow. Feel the warm relaxation.

"My Right Knee is completely relaxed."

See the glow. Feel the warm relaxation.

"My Left Thigh is completely relaxed."

See the glow. Feel the warm relaxation.

"My Right Thigh is completely relaxed."

See the glow. Feel the warm relaxation.

"My Pelvic Girdle, Crotch and Buttocks are completely relaxed."

See the glow. Feel the warm relaxation.

"From the Waist down, my entire lower body is completely relaxed and at peace."

See your entire lower body glowing with the soft white light, and feel it all feeling completely relaxed, warm and comfortable.

"My Stomach is completely relaxed."

See the glow. Feel the warm relaxation.

"My Chest is completely relaxed."

See the glow. Feel the warm relaxation.

"My Left Shoulder is completely relaxed."

See the glow. Feel the warm relaxation.

"My Right Shoulder is completely relaxed."

See the glow. Feel the warm relaxation.

"My Left Upper Arm is completely relaxed."

See the glow. Feel the warm relaxation.

"My Right Upper Arm is completely relaxed."

See the glow. Feel the warm relaxation.

"My Left Elbow is completely relaxed."

See the glow. Feel the warm relaxation.

"My Right Elbow is completely relaxed."

See the glow. Feel the warm relaxation.

"My Left Forearm is completely relaxed."

See the glow. Feel the warm relaxation.

"My Right Forearm is completely relaxed."

See the glow. Feel the warm relaxation.

"My Left Wrist is completely relaxed."

See the glow. Feel the warm relaxation.

"My Right Wrist is completely relaxed."

See the glow. Feel the warm relaxation.

"My Left Hand is completely relaxed."

See the glow. Feel the warm relaxation.

"My Right Hand is completely relaxed."

See the glow. Feel the warm relaxation.

"My Lower Back and Spine are completely relaxed."

See the glow. Feel the warm relaxation.

"My Upper Back and Spine are completely relaxed."

See the glow. Feel the warm relaxation.

"My Neck is completely relaxed."

See the glow. Feel the warm relaxation.

"From the Neck down, my entire body is totally and completely relaxed. I feel very comfortable, warm, safe and secure, and I am completely relaxed."

"The Back of my Head is completely relaxed."

See the glow. Feel the warm relaxation.

"The Top of my Head is completely relaxed."

See the glow. Feel the warm relaxation.

"The Left Side of my Head is completely relaxed."

See the glow. Feel the warm relaxation.

"The Right Side of my Head is completely relaxed."

See the glow. Feel the warm relaxation.

"My Face is completely relaxed."

See the glow. Feel the warm relaxation.

"My Entire Head is completely relaxed."

See the glow. Feel the warm relaxation.

"My Whole Body is now utterly and totally relaxed and

at peace. I feel completely comfortable and relaxed, and I am already in a light hypnotic state."

See yourself, in your current position, glowing with healing, soothing white light. Feel yourself totally and completely relaxed, both mentally and physically.

"Now that I have relaxed my body, I am going to do the same for my mind, and in the process, I will take myself further into this lovely hypnotic trance. I am going to count from 20 down to 1, and with each number that I count, I will gently slip deeper and deeper into a warm, relaxing, welcoming hypnotic state which I, and only I, control."

"20."

"19."

"18."

"17."

"16. Already I can feel my mind slipping into a beautiful, warm trance."

"15."

"14."

"13."

"12."

"11. My trance is deepening and deepening, and I am gently going into a deep, powerful hypnotic state."

"10."

"9."

"8."

"7."

"6. I am nearly there now, feeling completely comfortable, safe and at peace."

"5."

"4."

"3."

"2. I am just about to fall into a beautiful, safe, relaxed trance so that I can work to heal myself."

"1."

At this point, you will now be deeply relaxed, and whether you are aware of it or not, in a strong self-hypnotic trance. To actually work in this state is just as simple as it was getting yourself into it. You speak a declaration of what you wish to be true, phrasing it as if it were already the case. This is called an affirmation. At the same time, construct a mental picture of yourself in a situation where this new truth is completely self-evident; such as you not being in pain, having normal, regular bowel movements, eating without feeling discomfort or bloating, or whatever your particular IBS symptoms are.

Below this paragraph, I will give you a list of affirmations that will deal with all the symptoms of IBS; simply pick out the ones that address your particular problems, or if you like, construct your own affirmations, as long as you remember to keep them present tense, and phrased so as to imply that the desired state of affairs is actually the case. You will see exactly what I mean when you read the affirmations.

The final point about the affirmations is that you should speak each one three times, and as you do so, feel its truth, know that you are speaking the simple truth (you won't be, but soon you will be, so ignore the fact that to begin with, it won't be true, and believe it anyway), and picture yourself in a scene where it is true. If you do this, you will notice positive effects within two weeks, and within a month you will be starting to forget how nasty IBS was.

The affirmations are:

General: "I do not suffer in any way from Irritable Bowel Syndrome."

Pain: "I am free from all of the pain associated with

Irritable Bowel Syndrome. IBS causes me no discomfort."

Constipation: "My bowel movements are regular and occur on a daily basis. I never have any trouble evacuating my bowels."

Diarrhoea: "My bowel movements are regular and occur once a day. They are always fully voluntary, and they are always firm and healthy. I always feel the need to defecate build up slowly and gently."

Faecal Mucus: "My stools are always firm and healthy, and never carry excess mucus."

Bloating: "The gas that I ingest as part of daily life is minimal, and is processed rapidly and effectively by my digestive system without leaving me in any discomfort."

Intestinal Noise: "My digestive system is efficient, regular and quiet."

Flatulence/Belching: "Any gas that I may swallow as part of everyday life is quickly dissipated naturally by my digestive system. I never involuntarily eject wind either orally or anally."

Nausea: "My stomach is calm and settled at all times. I never feel queasy, and do not suffer from nausea."

Lack of Appetite: "My body always tells me how

much food it needs me to consume, and I am always happy to do so. My appetite is healthy and normal, without being excessive."

Indigestion/Heartburn: "My stomach secretes the amount of acid that is necessary to efficiently digest my food, and only that. All of these gastric fluids stay within the confines of my digestive system, and cause me no discomfort. My digestion works normally and effectively."

General Stress: "I have a strong mind. Very few things worry me, and I am very slow to get irritated or frustrated. While I do not neglect things which I need to do, their presence does not make me fret. I am peaceful, healthy, and stress-free."

Lack of Energy/Weakness: "I am an energetic, healthy and hearty person. My body is strong, and I never suffer from a lack of energy or from spells of physical weakness or lassitude. I am an energetic, vital person at all times."

Faintness: "My circulatory system is healthy and effective, and my digestion provides my blood with all the energy and nutrients that it needs. I never feel faint or dizzy."

Palpitations: "My heartbeat is strong, regular and healthy at all times. It does not waver, palpitate, fibrillate or deviate from its natural beat. My heart is a healthy, natural, and finely-toned muscle."

Agitation: "I am a very calm person. Outside stresses and worries do not bother me. While I do not neglect my life or my problems, I find that I can consider them calmly and lucidly, without getting worried or upset."

Depression: "I am a very cheerful and outgoing person. I find my life fun and interesting, and I enjoy every moment of it, as well as looking forward to each new day. I am enthusiastic and happy."

The affirmations above will allow you to remove any particular symptom of Irritable Bowel Syndrome that you are troubled with. If you do not like any of the affirmations, make up your own. The pattern should be obvious to you. Also, if you want to deal with any other problems that you may have, create affirmations for them, too.

It may take you a little time to remember your affirmations by heart. Before your first session, choose which affirmations you want to use, and write them out on some paper. Once you have done this, until you can remember them, have them close to hand and convenient, and when you want to look at the sheet, say "I will now briefly open my eyes. This will not disturb my level of trance in the slightest", and go ahead and read the affirmation. If you have to do this for each one, then so be it. You will soon learn them.

It will also help speed up the process if you keep the sheet by your bed at night, and say the affirmations to yourself just before you go to sleep and when you first wake up. Throw all the belief and enthusiasm that you can into this, but do not bother to put yourself into a trance.

Once you have finished reading your affirmations, then you will want to bring yourself comfortably back out of the trance. This is done in the reverse way to going in, but is much shorter. To do this, say the following out loud:

"I am about to count to three and click my fingers. When I do so, I will awake from this trance feeling calm, refreshed and healthy. My problems with IBS will be greatly relieved, and I will be much easier to hypnotise the next time."

"1."

"2."

"3."

And click your fingers. The trance session is over, and should have taken slightly under 30 minutes from start to finish. If you cannot click your fingers, then substitute a wiggle of them instead, but in actual movement, and in the text above.

EXPECTED RESULTS

Self-hypnosis of this sort should be performed daily, and you will see the effects of it 10-14 days after starting, with complete effect taking hold after about a month. At this point, you may like to switch to just the general affirmation against IBS for a further two or three weeks before stopping entirely. If the symptoms should ever recur, then start the self-hypnosis again. After six weeks of it, you will probably have come to enjoy it as a nice, relaxing way of spending some time. Any time you wish, you can hypnotise yourself, and just let yourself drift for a while without making affirmations. It is a wonderful way of refreshing and revitalising yourself, and it beats watching television!

SECTION 5

Other Forms of Healing and IBS

Irritable Bowel Syndrome responds well to most forms of alternative healing, to a greater or lesser degree. The two forms that are especially effective with this particular disease are homoeopathy and acupuncture.

HOMOEOPATHY

Homoeopathy is the modern interpretation of the ancient art of herbal healing as practised for thousands of years throughout the world. The art is based on the premise that "Like Cures Like", the law of sympathy. In homoeopathy, the body is considered to be made up of four different elements, or 'humours' – black bile, yellow bile, phlegm and cholic – each of which has to be in equal balance to lead to health. All diseases are seen as an imbalance of one or more of the humours, and the nature of the problem will show which one. This is then cross-referenced against the area of the body, and the specifics of the symptoms, to reveal the correct treatment for the illness.

Much to the surprise of the modern medical profession, homoeopathy has proven itself to be an extremely effective form of treatment for a wide variety of problems, including Irritable Bowel Syndrome, and it is starting to see regular use alongside conventional medicines in many health services worldwide. It has a further benefit in that unlike many of the artificial drugs that doctors prescribe, homoeopathic treatments very rarely have any side-effects whatsoever, other than to make you well again.

Homoeopathic healers are now fairly easy to find in most large towns, and even some small ones, and in many places you will have a selection to choose from. There are several bodies worldwide that certify that a particular healer has passed certain levels of training, and is of an acceptable level of ability, so it is well worth asking any given healer that you consider using for evidence of certification. The only ones that will take even the slightest offence are those who do not legitimately have such qualifications. The cost varies widely, from healer to healer as well as from location to location, so you may find that it is worth your while doing a little shopping around.

ACUPUNCTURE

Acupuncture, although of the same sort of age as homoeopathy, could not be much more different. Acupuncture is based on the belief that the health of the body is dependent on the correct flow of an internal energy, called Chi. The Chi in your body powers all of your cells and organs, and so it has to be able to flow correctly to all areas in order for you to be healthy and fit. Furthermore, this energy network is mirrored on the skin of the body, and so any deficiencies or blocks in the flow of Chi will produce blockages in the energy on the skin. The lines of energy cross frequently, and meet at junctions, so there is a complete web on the skin. By lightly pricking the skin at certain junctions of lines, Chi flow in the body can be adjusted and corrected, and so diseases (which are all caused by Chi imbalance) can be cured.

Acupuncture has as good a track record as homoeopathy, if not better, achieving cure rates that are of the same order as conventional medical treatment, and it is particularly good in curing Irritable Bowel Syndrome. During acupuncture, once the problem has been identified, small needles are placed into your skin at the appropriate location. The needles are placed so lightly and so shallowly that you have to be particularly sensitive to even feel them; there is very little pain involved, save at one or two specific energy junctions which are very rarely used. Any acupuncturist without evidence of having completed the very strict courses (often many years long) involved in learning the art of Chinese Healing ought to be completely avoided.

Acupuncture is a very powerful and effective form of healing, and it will completely alleviate Irritable Bowel Syndrome in the majority of cases.

There are of course many other forms of alternative treatments that you can obtain, such as aromatherapy, crystal healing, colour therapy, iridology and psychic surgery, and in most cases they can help, but I specifically recommend homoeopathy and acupuncture, along with the other methods of healing detailed in this book: Meditation, Pranic Breathing, Flotation Therapy and Self-Hypnosis.

These forms of healing have all proven time and time again to help many hundreds of thousands of IBS sufferers back to a normal, comfortable lifestyle, free from the effects of this debilitating disease.

"After 30 years of foot problems – something that ACTUALLY WORKS!"

SOOTHE YOUR SORE ACHING FEET!

Which of these foot ailments cause you pain?

- ☐ **CORNS**
- ☐ **CALLUSES**
- ☐ **BUNIONS**
- ☐ **FLAT FEET**
- ☐ **PAIN IN THE BALLS OF THE FEET**
- ☐ **CRAMPS IN THE FEET AND TOES**
- ☐ **PAIN IN THE HEEL**
- ☐ **PAINFUL ANKLES**
- ☐ **ACHING LEGS**

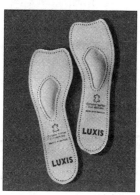

If you suffer from one or more of these problems, then you owe it to yourself to try the remarkable LUXIS LEATHER INSOLES. They are an amazing discovery from Europe, and we will guarantee a full refund if LUXIS LEATHER INSOLES do not soothe your aching feet immediately.

LUXIS' specially designed metatarsal support helps your feet assume their proper posture and balance. They help redistribute your body weight naturally, thereby relieving painful uneven pressures that can cause sore burning feet, corns, calluses, bunions, sore heels or ankles and foot problems of all types.

It's a proven fact that aching feet can also be the cause of pain in the legs, knees and back.

Like other foot pain sufferers you may have tried new shoes, shop bought inserts or supports with little or no relief from your foot pain.

"I had sore feet for a long time, but not anymore thanks to your insoles."
E.S., Lancaster, PA

Don't despair! LUXIS LEATHER INSOLES are now available at an affordable price and WE GUARANTEE A REFUND IF LUXIS LEATHER INSOLES DO NOT RELIEVE YOUR ACHING FEET AS SOON AS YOU PUT THEM ON.

LUXIS LEATHER INSOLES are contoured to give your feet the necessary metatarsal support they need to restore proper balance and are specially constructed to relieve pressure and add gentle support to the arch of your foot. A cushiony soft pad in LUXIS LEATHER INSOLES absorbs shock. These amazing insoles shape themselves to your feet for a true customized fit.

"The insoles are fantastic. I've suffered with foot problems all my life. Suddenly, I can walk in comfort."
L.C., White Plains, NY

LUXIS LEATHER INSOLES are handcrafted from 100% sheep leather which lets your feet breathe naturally. They are soft, long wearing, absorbent and conform to your feet. These insoles are not available at any price in any shop but only through this special limited mail-order offer.

Once you slip a pair into your shoes, you'll never want to walk without them. Your toes will uncurl, pressure will disappear and every step will be a pleasure.

Pamper your feet with the all-day comfort that only genuine LUXIS LEATHER INSOLES provide. So thin and light you can wear them in any shoes.

30 DAY NO - RISK OFFER

Try LUXIS LEATHER INSOLES for 30 days. If you are not 100% satisfied, simply return them for a prompt full refund of your purchase price. What could be more fair!

"Vinegar
Nature's secret weapon"

by Maxwell Stein

You'll find vinegar in just about every kitchen in the country – but most of us only ever use it on chips or as a salad dressing. Did you know there are hundreds of other uses for vinegar? In his incredible new book, Maxwell Stein looks at how vinegar has been used around the home and as a traditional remedy. If you thought vinegar was just used for salad dressing... then you're in for a big surprise!

"Vinegar – nature's secret weapon" is a new book in which the author looks at over 325 tried and tested uses for vinegar. For example, Maxwell checks out how vinegar has been used to:

- Polish the chrome on the car
- Clean work surfaces, mirrors and glass
- Repair scratches in wood
- Whiten whites, brighten colours and fade sweat stains
- Ease the pain of insect bites
- Lift stains on carpets
- Remove ink stains
- Clean brass, copper and pewter
- Banish unpleasant odours
- Dissolve chewing gum
- And much, much more.

Maxwell also tells us why he thinks vinegar can be used to:

- Soothe tired and aching feet
- Relieve headaches
- Lift painful corns and calluses
- Clear embarrassing dandruff
- Help treat burns
- Help fade age spots
- Prevent infections
- Ease nausea and stomach upset
- Relieve coughs and tickly throats
- Cure hiccups – fast
- Relieve a sore throat
- Guard against food poisoning
- Disinfect almost anything – it's used in many hospitals
- Soothe painful sunburn

Over 325 different uses in total. But that's not all, Maxwell also covers Honey and Garlic and tells you why he believes they are both powerful natural allies of vinegar.

Honey and Garlic too!

As a special bonus and for a limited time only, we have included two completely free sections to the Vinegar book – so, not only do you get a Vinegar book, but you also get a Honey book and Garlic book too – that's three of nature's secret wonders all for just £9.95.

You'll see how Maxwell put these three natural wonders to the test as he looks at many common ailments. He talks about how honey and garlic have been used as simple, yet cost effective home remedies – alone or mixed with vinegar <u>and</u> at a fraction of what you'd pay for commercially prepared products.

In these two special BONUS sections of *"Vinegar, – nature's secret weapon"*, Maxwell looks at many health problems and whether simple treatments can be used to tackle them, such as:

- An easy poultice which has been used to treat painful joints
- A simple drink used to ease muscle pain fast!
- An easy to prepare mixture to prevent burns from scarring
- A tasty recipe, used to help keep cholesterol at a healthy level
- A fast remedy used to treat cold sores
- A morning treat to ease the discomfort of asthma
- An ancient Indian broth, used for blood pressure
- Delicious tea used to add sparkle to dull sex lives
- A tasty brew that has been used to help lose weight
- A method used to stop toothache by relieving pain naturally
- A Russian folk remedy, used to treat colds
- A fast method for clearing spots and blemishes
- A simple method to ease gas and indigestion problems fast
- A preparation which has been used to combat the flu

And many, many more health questions answered.

These special bonus sections on Honey & Garlic are only available for a limited time, so to avoid disappointment, please send your order now – and you'll be getting three for the price of one. All with a full, three month money back guarantee.

To order *"Vinegar, Honey & Garlic – nature's secret weapons"*, simply complete the coupon below.

Relief from Restless Legs Syndrome

IF **YOU** have trouble falling asleep or sitting because of uncomfortable sensations in your legs accompanied by an irresistible urge to move, you may suffer from Restless Legs Syndrome (RLS). A new handbook has just been released that reveals how to get all-natural relief from this condition.

This handbook – *Stopping Restless Legs Syndrome* – reveals the latest, up-to-date facts on RLS – what causes symptoms, how to get rid of them using all-natural means, and how to protect yourself from RLS distress.

The handbook reveals specific facts on new natural, alternative and medical remedies, that bring fast relief without the use of potentially dangerous drugs.

You'll discover what foods and activities to avoid at all costs, specific nutrients you should add to your diet, the impact of gentle massage and stretching, a vitamin and herb supplement that increases circulation in the legs and promotes healing, specific pressure points that bring almost instant relief and a simple isometric exercise to do before bedtime that has brought relief to thousands of sufferers – along with much more.

The handbook gives you a full explanation of RLS – in plain English – and why millions of people suffer from this condition.

Many people are suffering from RLS symptoms because they do not know of the new all-natural treatments revealed in this handbook. Get the facts!

Order today using the freephone number below or by sending the coupon. You have three whole months to try this book. If you are not completely satisfied, return it and you'll get a full refund – no questions asked.

Get relief from Fibromyalgia

Natural Alternative and Medical Solutions

A NEW BOOK reveals how to get relief from Fibromyalgia symptoms such as **chronic muscle pain, fatigue, memory or concentration problems, sleeping problems, headaches, numbness and tingling, and sensitivity to cold.**

The *Fibromyalgia Relief Handbook* reveals the latest information on Fibromyalgia – why its specific cause is not known, how it can best be treated and how to protect yourself from troublesome symptoms.

This book gives you specific facts on the brand new natural, alternative and medical solutions that can bring prompt and welcome relief.

You'll discover specific measures to deal with "hurting all over", tender spots, getting a good night's sleep, irritable bowel problems, and the other symptoms associated with Fibromyalgia.

The book reveals what foods help the condition, what you should know about the nutrients calcium and magnesium and what to avoid at all costs. You'll even discover the benefits of therapeutic massage relaxation and meditation techniques, exercise – and much more.

The book gives you a full explanation of Fibromyalgia – in plain English – and why so many people suffer from it.

Many people are suffering from Fibromyalgia symptoms because they do not know where to find safe and appropriate treatment. Get all the facts.

To order your copy of the *Fibromyalgia Relief Handbook*, complete and post the coupon below or call our Freephone Orderline on the number below.